Create Your Research Poster

Sara Miller McCune founded SAGE Publishing in 1965 to support the dissemination of usable knowledge and educate a global community. SAGE publishes more than 1000 journals and over 800 new books each year, spanning a wide range of subject areas. Our growing selection of library products includes archives, data, case studies and video. SAGE remains majority owned by our founder and after her lifetime will become owned by a charitable trust that secures the company's continued independence.

Los Angeles | London | New Delhi | Singapore | Washington DC | Melbourne

SUPER
QUICK
SKILLS

Create Your Research Poster

Corina Lacatus
Alex Nogues

Los Angeles | London | New Delhi
Singapore | Washington DC | Melbourne

Los Angeles | London | New Delhi
Singapore | Washington DC | Melbourne

SAGE Publications Ltd
1 Oliver's Yard
55 City Road
London EC1Y 1SP

SAGE Publications Inc.
2455 Teller Road
Thousand Oaks, California 91320

SAGE Publications India Pvt Ltd
B 1/I 1 Mohan Cooperative Industrial Area
Mathura Road
New Delhi 110 044

SAGE Publications Asia-Pacific Pte Ltd
3 Church Street
#10-04 Samsung Hub
Singapore 049483

Editor: Jai Seaman
Editorial assistant: Hannah Cavender-Deere
Production editor: Tanya Szwarnowska
Proofreader: Aud Scriven
Marketing manager: Catherine Slinn
Cover design: Shaun Mercier
Typeset by: C&M Digitals (P) Ltd, Chennai, India

Library of Congress Control Number: 2021932391

British Library Cataloguing in Publication data

A catalogue record for this book is available from the British Library

ISBN 978-1-5297-6757-5

At SAGE we take sustainability seriously. Most of our products are printed in the UK using responsibly sourced papers and boards. When we print overseas we ensure sustainable papers are used as measured by the PREPS grading system. We undertake an annual audit to monitor our sustainability.

Contents

Everything in this book!

Section 1   Why do we need research posters?

Being asked to create a poster can be confusing. You will learn why research posters are important and why you are asked to create them.

Section 2   Which elements of my project should I include in my research poster?

Understanding how to communicate your research through posters becomes easier when you make some decisions about content early. Here you can learn the main steps to get off to a good start.

Section 3   What does a good research poster look like?

This section is packed with essential information about the main visual and content elements that make a very good poster.

Section 4   What do I need to think about before creating my poster?

Getting the practical information right at the start makes poster design much easier, so here are the questions to ask before you begin working on your own poster.

Section 5   How do I get going with visualizing my research?

Getting started is often challenging, so here you will find practical advice on how you can generate graphs and visual representations of the main parts of your research.

Section 6   How do I tell the right story with my poster?

A research poster tells a story about your research to a wider audience. Here you will find out what you need to do to tell a compelling story with your own poster.

Section 7   How do I use images?

Here you will find lots of practical tips about how to select and use relevant images and illustrations for your poster.

Section 8   How do I know if my poster is good?

This section will give you different checklists and templates to help you make decisions about the content of your poster and to enable you to design a good poster.

Section 9   How do I integrate my research poster in a good presentation?

Often, you will be asked to present your poster and/or to address questions about it, and this section offers advice on how to prepare well for such situations.

Why do we need research posters?

*10 second
summary*

Being asked to create a poster can be
confusing. Learn why research posters
are important and why you are asked to
create them.

60 second summary

Sometimes it is difficult to wrap your head around the purpose of creating a research poster. After all, why should posters matter when often you engage in research that is not visual in nature? This section explains why research posters are important for your learning. Firstly, they can visually communicate your research to wider audiences, like fellow students, staff members, or the wider community. Secondly, teachers can consider them a type of assessment of your learning, included as a marked or unmarked assignment in individual classes, or as a more creative way to judge your progress with dissertation research and writing.

The premise of research posters

A research poster communicates your work to your peers and instructors, relying on a mix of images and text. In a sense, posters bring your research papers to life. Hence, you have more freedom to choose colours, images, illustrations in addition to the text you want to share with your audience.

Sometimes you might be asked to present the content of the poster to your audience, sometimes you may have to let the poster 'speak for itself'. When done well, posters can tell a coherent and compelling story about your work, motivating the audience to ask questions and engage in conversation with you about your research. However interestingly, a written paper is likely to have only very few readers (usually your instructor, tutor, or course convenor, and possibly a friend you may have asked to read the paper as a personal favour).

The conversations you have with a wider audience looking at your poster usually result in comments and suggestions that can help you improve and develop your research further.

You might be asked to present your poster as:

1   A stand-alone poster, often included in a poster exhibition or perhaps uploaded online.
2   A poster presentation, as part of a class event or in a 'poster session'.

You might be asked to prepare your poster:

1   Alone, as part of an individual assignment.
2   With fellow students, as part of a group assignment.

Depending on the expectations about how to create and present a poster, some will find the process a bit challenging while others will find it stimulating and creative.

Answer these questions to gauge how you feel about creating a research poster. If you have concerns about creating posters and presenting them, answering these questions may help you identify the main sources of your fear and the best ways to address them.

What are you looking forward to the most about creating your poster?

What are your greatest fears (if any) about creating a poster?

What can you do to reduce your concerns (if any)?

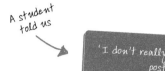

'I don't really understand the point of doing a poster about my research.'

A poster is a creative way to communicate your research and gather feedback on it.

Why are students asked to create posters?

There are two main goals:

- To disseminate information about your research to your peers as well as tutors and possibly also a wider audience.

- To assess your learning, progress with research.

Posters will often include the following types of information about your research:

- Work in progress (intended to further your learning and assist with developing your work further).

- Completed research (intended to share finished work with a wider audience and to assess learning at the end of a course/once learning has completed).

Posters as assessment

1 Course assessment

Tutors may ask you to create research posters as a type of assessment included in a course (in addition to an essay or a written exam). Depending on the course, you might receive a mark for it, or you might simply receive oral or written feedback without a mark.

2 Dissertation assessment

Many degree programmes require you to create a 'dissertation poster' to present your progress or completed work on your dissertation. You may also be expected to offer a presentation that explains the main elements or to display your poster in a 'poster session' that is open to your peers, your dissertation supervisor, other members of your department, and possibly the entire university community. As with posters created as part of a course, dissertation posters can present work in progress, with the intention of gathering feedback and suggestions for improvement, or they can present completed work, celebrating the accomplishment of finishing your dissertation.

ACTIVITY

Before you begin developing your poster, make sure that you gather and understand all the information about the following:

1. The main reasons why you have been asked to create a research poster.

2. The type of information you are expected to include.

3. How you will be assessed on the poster.

'The power of posters rests in their capacity to make an immediate impact on the audience.'

What is the relevance of research posters in the academic community?

- **Time efficiency:** More people can quickly learn about your research.

- **Open engagement:** Given the visual nature of posters, they can allow more people to have access to your work, learn from it, and offer feedback.

- **Stimulate learning:** Preparing a poster compels you to formulate your research in clear and concise ways, which is often a great way to develop it further.

- **Employability:** Posters prepare students for professional life, as they are widely used across disciplines in academia and also in different domains of activity outside of academia: in research-focused posts in government, international organizations, and the private sector.

Evaluate the four goals of research poster design in their order of relevance, as they apply to your own research poster.

	High relevance	Medium relevance	Low relevance	No relevance
Time efficiency				
Open engagement				
Stimulate learning				
Employability				

Explain why some goals might be more or less relevant than others, in the case of your particular research poster.

....

....

....

Which elements of my project should I include in my research poster?

10 second summary

Understanding how to communicate your research through posters becomes easier when you make some decisions about content early on. Let's learn the main steps to get off to a good start.

60 second summary

One of the most important steps in research poster design is at the very start of the process, when you have to make some key decisions about which parts of your research are worth sharing with others and what information might be well-suited for a poster. Of course, the research-related information you choose to include in your poster will depend in large part on the stage you have reached with your research. This section offers you practical tips on how to plan your thinking and structure your research to increase your chances of making informed decisions about what belongs on a poster and what does not.

Main elements of research design

All research projects are different. Some test theory and some build theory, while some make use of quantitative data, and others use qualitative data. Regardless of preference, all research in the social sciences contain some essential constitutive elements. In other words, all research projects follow specific research designs, which is a strategy that integrates different components of a study in a coherent and logical way, with their own research questions, argument, theoretical and analytical frameworks, and analysis.

To build a good poster, you need to make sure that you have a research design for your project and at least some of the key elements of the project in place. You need not have all the elements ready or finalized (i.e. you might not have all your data collected, for instance) by the time you design your poster, as you can always focus on the information you have. However, it's always a good idea to have a good sense of the overall structure of the project before you plan your poster.

Qualitative data
Generally non-numerical data obtained by the researcher from sources such as first-hand observation, interviews, questionnaires and focus groups.

Quantitative data
Numerical data that can be statistically analysed.

The main elements of a research project/design:

- A clearly defined research interest/topic.

- A 'gap' in scholarship that you are seeking to fill with your research.

- A research question.

- A body of academic work to which you aim to contribute with your research (and which you review, discuss, and position your research against).

- Research hypotheses or research expectations and argument (i.e. not all types of research use hypotheses, as is the case with most types of research using qualitative data).

- A method of data collection and analysis and a justification for it being the best-suited to answer your research question.

- Data, a data collection strategy, and a method of analysis (i.e. most, but not all types of research make use of data, such as theoretical research).

- Analysis and discussion of findings.

- A conclusion.

CHECK POINT

Use the checklist below to figure out where you are at in your research as you begin working on your research poster. Tick off any of the steps you have already completed:

- ☐ Research interest/topic.

- ☐ 'Gap' in scholarship.

- ☐ Research question.

- ☐ A body of academic work which you aim to contribute to.

- ☐ Research hypotheses/research expectations and argument (as relevant for your research).

- ☐ Method of data collection and methodology.

- ☐ Data, and method of analysis (if applicable).

- ☐ Analysis and discussion of findings.

- ☐ Conclusion.

Brainstorming about the research poster and its content

Brainstorming is an informal approach to problem solving to come up with ideas and solutions about the text, images, and composition of your poster. You can brainstorm with fellow students, but you can also brainstorm alone. It is important to remain non-judgmental and to welcome all ideas at this stage.

Choose a topic that's different from your research, for example 'The rise of electric cars' or 'Artificial intelligence in everyday life'. Then give yourself no more than one or two minutes to quickly sketch the composition of a poster, keeping it very high level.

1 Repeat at least once more, trying to do it differently, and compare your sketches. Which one do you think is the best and why?

2 Repeat this with your own research topic.

This activity helps you think about the main parts and how best to arrange them. Small details can wait. There is no right or wrong way to draw here and you certainly do not need to know how to draw well. Think 'stick figures' and simple lines for this exercise.

'Not all ideas are made to be researched, but all research builds on a distillation of new and old ideas.'

Making decisions about the main elements of your poster

At this early stage of planning, you have a good idea of the stage you have reached with your research. It may be a good idea to set some general goals for your poster, which can help offer some direction to your thinking and planning.

Take some time to think about the following two questions. They will help you define a purpose for the poster that is unique to you and your project. Their answers will inform your next decisions about the poster, as explained in later sections of this book.

1. What kind of feedback do you want to get out of presenting your research as a poster?

2. What are the areas on which you want to get feedback?

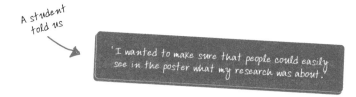

A student told us

'I wanted to make sure that people could easily see in the poster what my research was about.'

While all parts of your research are important, some will always be more important than others when it comes to conveying your message. It is for you to find out which ones they are and treat them accordingly.

Examples

In the following sections, you will get the chance to learn how to make informed decisions about the different components of your poster. For now, what matters is to begin to think about the research elements and how important they might be. This will help you decide:

1 Whether or not they should be included in the poster at all.
2 Whether they should occupy a prominent or a secondary position.

Research design
The overall strategy that researchers use to integrate different components of a study in a coherent and logical way.

Let us take two main elements of research design and think about their role and position on the poster. For instance, you might decide that a graph presenting some of your findings belongs in a place that is very visible, like the top centre of your poster.

Research question
A question that a research project sets out to answer.

The research question

Where does it belong on the poster?

- At the very top?
- In the centre of the poster?
- At the bottom of the poster?

Why did you pick a certain position versus another?

The 'gap' in scholarship

What information will you include to help the audience understand what previous scholarship you are seeking to contribute to?

- Will you include any names of scholars or quotes?
- Will you include any graphs or images to illustrate previous scholarship?

Why have you made this choice?

How will you explain the 'gap' to which you aim to contribute to the audience?

- Will you include an image?
- Will you use written text?

Why have you used a particular text or image to explain the 'gap'?

Congratulations

You have made great progress understanding the main elements of your research project and making important decisions about which ones you would like to include in your poster. These are key elements for planning. Now you are ready to learn how best to make your research visual and turn it into a research poster.

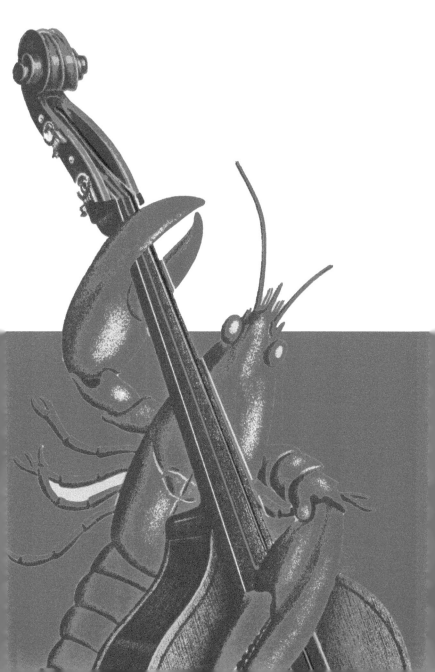

What does a good research poster look like?

10 second summary

This section is packed with essential information about the main visual and content elements that make a good poster.

60 second summary

Your research poster is, first and foremost, a visual piece of work. Getting acquainted with some foundational rules of visual design will be very useful when you make key decisions about your poster. The good news is that you will only need a few basics to maximize results. This chapter will get you thinking about the right structure for your research poster and how to create a compelling visual representation for that research. It will help you make informed decisions about how you can best communicate the broader structure of your research, in a visual form that is compelling and easy to understand.

Basic visuals and composition

We instinctively organize information to make sense of layers and hier-archies. For instance, in English (and other Indo-European languages) we learn to read from left to right (and top to bottom). We thus 'train' our brain to read most other messaging this way; also when we look at a poster and try to understand the information represented on it. This tends to be true for digital and printed material.

Our eyes also respond to differences in visual weight (we say one element is visually heavier than another when it is more promi-nent and thus more likely to be noticed).

Visual weight
The notion that factors like colour or size can render design elements more visually prominent than others.

Factors that can alter the visual weight of an element are:

- Size – an object/element being larger than the next.

- Colour – some colours catch our eye more, and a combination of bright and dark tones will stand out more than, say, two similar shades of grey.

- Shape – certain shapes can stand out more than others, for instance, a star is generally seen as more interesting than a square).

Visual weight difference

By size

By colour and lightness

By shape

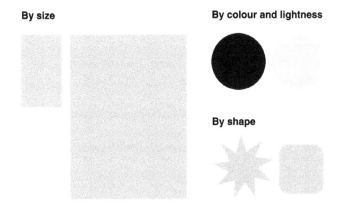

Symmetry is another way to play with composition and make it more dynamic. Generally, symmetric alignments tend to be perceived as more 'static' and less 'eye-catching'. Don't force yourself to use asymmetry for the sake of it, but it is something to take into account depending on how you intend to present your work. There is no need to give all elements the same room if you consider some are more important than others. See the image below: the composition on the right is more interesting, partly because it immediately gives us clues as to where to look first (what is more important).

The main rules of visual composition

You do not need to know these rules by heart, but they are good to be aware of, and will help you figure out ways to help your audience make sense of the content you're presenting. They will also help you when revising and improving your poster.

Law of proximity: Elements that are near, or proximate to each other, tend to be grouped together. Because the circles on the left are close to each other, we instinctively assume they belong together.

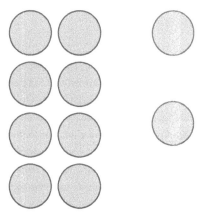

Law of similarity: We perceive similar elements as a complete picture, shape, or group, even when those elements are separated. For example, we'd think of the blue circles as a group rather than just scattered dots.

Law of common region: When elements share an area with a clearly defined boundary they tend to be perceived as belonging to a group.

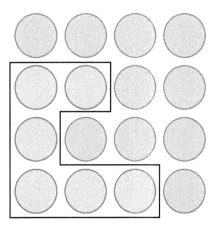

The isolation effect: When elements are similar, the one standing out is most likely to be remembered.

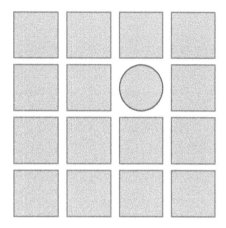

The serial position effect: People tend to best remember the first and last items in a series.

Law of connection: Elements that are visually connected are perceived as more related than elements with no connection.

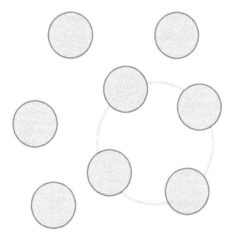

Breathing space: margins are your friends. Cram too many elements without some padding around them and things will end up looking too busy, discouraging your audience. Think of space proportionally to each element to keep things tidy (and when it comes to text, the right interlining will contribute to readability).

CHECK
POINT

Which of these rules are more likely to influence how you organize the elements of your research poster?

- [ ] Law of proximity.

- [ ] Law of similarity.

- [ ] Law of common region.

- [ ] The isolation effect.

- [ ] The serial position effect.

- [ ] Law of connection.

- [ ] Breathing space.

Why have you selected these laws in particular?

The quick view vs the long view

Inevitably, many may just walk by, while others may spend longer exploring your poster; and they may have different levels of expertise or interest, so how to cater to all? Remember the poster isn't your research, but rather an artifact representing it. Not everything needs to be there (and that's a good thing).

What is the quick view?

Could you convey your message in two seconds? Research shows that our brains tend to 'scan' a composition, and form a general idea, before we even start reading. You may not have longer than a few seconds (or less) to lure some people into reading further. So, the quick view is the information layer that is easy to get 'at a glance'.

How can you arrange information on your poster for the quick view?

Movie posters are a good example of this principle: usually there is a big image to convey the general feeling of the movie, then the title, in case you're still interested, and then, for those who really want to know the details, the small print. Our eyes 'read' the first two in a couple of seconds.

What is the long view?

This is the layer of information for those who are willing to learn about your research choices and outcomes. This is your opportunity to hold their hands and walk them through a good summary of what your research is about, why it matters, and so on.

How can you arrange information on your poster for the long view?

We mentioned how movie posters quickly grab our attention. Now imagine you've seen the movie and have a couple of minutes to tell your friends what the film is about and why they should watch it.

That is the long view: a more detailed narrative for your audience, so they can feel like you're right there, telling them about the essentials of your research, firsthand.

How can you combine the quick and the long view?

We can use a simple rule that will keep our poster content-rich without putting viewers off with too much clutter.

Whether you decide on a portrait or landscape format, and different types of layout, remember how our brains are trained to look at things in a particular order.

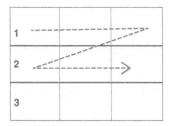 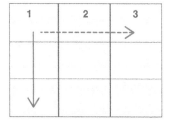

With this in mind, try to work with:

- One big focus, summarizing the most important theme (this is what you would tell someone if you had just a few seconds).

- Two to four contextual elements. More detailed information, adding nuance and context to your main claim (people should have a high level idea of your research after looking at these): what you did or tried to do, in which context, why it is important, what you found, etc.

- Additional details. These aren't essential to understanding, but contribute to back up your case, e.g. methodology, references, main figures, etc.

A student told us:

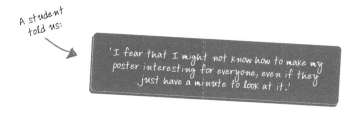

'I fear that I might not know how to make my poster interesting for everyone, even if they just have a minute to look at it.'

Fear not! There are simple ways to visually prioritize information to guide the audience's focus from the essential to the accessory.

Pick a format for your poster (*portrait* or *landscape)* and choose one of the basic layouts below (rows or columns). Then fill the spaces with some of the information you'd want to include, as well as the best wording for the headings for each section.

Why did you make these choices? Are there any advantages or disadvantages for what you want to communicate?

a		
b	b	b
c	c	c
c	c	c

a

b

c

c

b

c

c

b

c

c

Comparing examples

Find three examples of research posters online. Compare each one, noting what you like best and whether there is room for improvement. What can you say about them?

What do you like best about each poster?	Is there room for improvement anywhere?
1.	1.
2.	2.
3.	3.

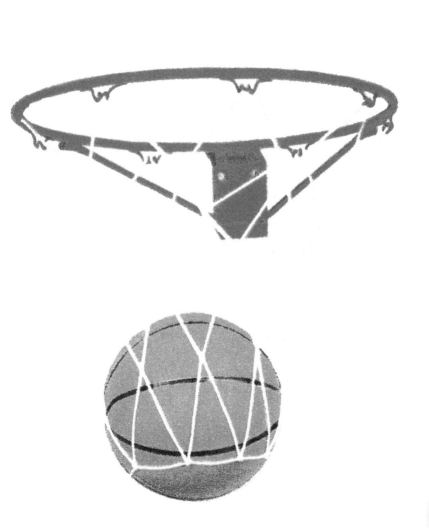

What do I need to think about before creating my poster?

10 second summary

Getting the practical information right at the start makes poster design much easier, so here are the questions to ask before you begin working on your own poster.

60 second summary

In addition to having a clear sense of where you are with your research and how you envision presenting it on a poster, there is some important practical information that is useful to have at this stage. Most course instructors and tutors (or conference organizers if you plan to participate in a poster session at a conference) will likely give you this information in preparation for your assignment. However, it can often happen, that you might be given only partial details. This session helps you identify the important practical information that you can ask for. Having this information will make your life much easier as you are designing your poster and getting it ready to be displayed.

Where will you be displaying your poster?

You are likely to have your poster on display in a place listed below (or somewhere similar):

- Small classroom.

- Large lecture theatre or a hall.

- Exhibition space.

- Dedicated large conference room.

Try to visit the space beforehand. If you do not have access to the space ahead of time, try to find out some details about it. Details about lighting, where your poster will be on display in the room and in relation to other posters will determine (in part!) the amount of content you might want to include, the way you will display the information, and the colours you will use for the different elements of the poster (you can find more details on these elements in the other sections of the book).

The goal is to make it easier for the audience to read and understand the content. Remember that most of the time your audience will have little time to dedicate to each individual poster and will likely be walking past your poster, trying to take in as much information as possible in just a matter of seconds. So, the more you help your audience see the most important information about your research, the better.

Often your course organizer or tutor will offer details about the recommended size of the poster. If the size of the poster is up to you, we recommend selecting a size that allows the reader to see the information well. Of course, there are also important considerations about price, availability of printing etc. that you will have to make, depending on your own personal circumstances.

The answers to the following questions will help you gather the relevant information:

- What size should my poster be?

- Could you recommend a certain printing service (perhaps available on campus and including student prices)?

- Where will my poster be on display?

- Will it be in direct light, or will the entire space be well-lit (or perhaps will have more diffuse light)?

- Will I have space to stand by the poster, to present it or address questions about it?

Online use

Sometimes, you may need (or choose to) display your poster online. In that case, readers will download the poster as an image or document and will read it on their computer/mobile screens. You do not want a file that is too heavy or unreadable (bulky files are more difficult to upload, share and explore, while excessive downsizing can lead to content becoming pixelated) and screen files are lighter than print files (lower resolution and size), so depending on what your audience may need:

- Think about where your poster will be hosted online (social media, email, etc.).

- Make a copy of your poster file (you don't want to lose the original).

- Export/save it as an image (PNG or JPEG and/or PDF), ideally reducing file size.

- Make sure the content can be read by zooming in. Ideally the file will be about 3MB or less.

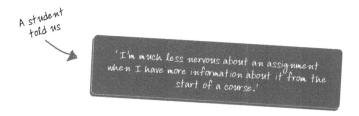

A student told us

'I'm much less nervous about an assignment when I have more information about it from the start of a course.'

Do ask questions, no matter how silly, or else you may put a lot of hard work into the wrong thing. Practical information will enable better choices and help you feel like you're off to a good start.

How much time do you have to prepare your poster?

More often than not, you will already know the display/submission date at the start of a course or at the time you are accepted into an event (conference or presentation). Sometimes you will also have all the details of the poster assignment included in the course handbook, or as a course material given to you at the start of term. This information will help you plan sufficient time for poster development, considering your progress on the research itself and other work and personal commitments you might have to complete during that time. The checklist on the next page will help you visualize and plan your work a bit better, allowing you to find room for poster planning. Tick off the steps you have completed.

☐ Get practical information (poster size, format, etc.).

☐ Check the venue and poster location if you can.

☐ Plan the logistics (printer availability and price, type of paper, etc.) and distribution if it needs to be seen online.

☐ Consider whether your audience is familiar with your field of research or not.

Who is your audience?

The core content of your poster will remain the same. However, you might choose to vary some elements, depending on your audience.

Display setting

Your audience will likely be made up of your fellow students and your course convenor or tutor. If your poster presents your dissertation research, your supervisor might also be in the audience, and other academic staff could also be present. You will need to make sure that you present the information on your poster in clear and concise academic terms. You will also want to include as many of the elements of your research as you have completed (see Section 2) and to do so in a clear and appealing manner.

If your poster will be on display in a setting where a non-academic audience is present, you might want to consider adding some more elements to your presentation that will 'translate' your research to the audience. While the core information about your research would remain the same, you might want to add some policy recommendations following from your research, if you will have policy-makers or members of the public and private sector in the audience.

ACTIVITY Break it down

1   What are the main sub-topics/themes you want to communicate?
    (e.g. if your main topic is linked to 'the rise of electric cars', sub-
    themes could be 'air quality', 'new means of transportation', 'battery
    technology', etc.).

2   Think about your audience's level of expertise on each of those
    sub-themes (e.g. advanced, intermediate or beginner), and how to
    best convey the message for each (i.e. text, images, tables/charts, a
    combination of all, etc.).

3   Add as many themes as you can and select only the most critical
    ones to tell your story on the poster.

This exercise is to show how sometimes concepts are easier to tackle
and solve when broken down into smaller pieces. The following sections
will offer even more details on how to select the information to include in
the poster, as linked to your research poster.

Is your project single-authored or developed in collaboration with one or several colleagues?

The processes of working as part of a group (to carry out research and create a poster which presents that research) are different when working as part of a group. Your research project will still have to contain all the elements of research design presented in Section 2, and your research poster design process will still follow the same criteria presented in this book, but the collaboration with one or more students will give the process different dynamics.

In a nutshell, you will have to consult with your fellow student partner(s) and make decisions about the research and the poster together. You will need to divide the work fairly and ensure that you communicate well. The details of the pros and cons of group work are beyond the scope of this book, but you can read about these in the dedicated book *Work Well in Groups* in the Super Quick Skills series.

What is the intended outcome of the research poster presentation?

The outcome of the presentation will impact on your choices. It might be:

- Assessment of coursework.

- Gaining peer feedback.

- Disseminating research findings to a wider non-academic audience.

'Let your research poster do most of the talking.'

How do I get going with visualizing my research?

10 second summary

Some hands-on, practical aspects are often challenging, so here you will find advice on picking the right tools and visual representations of the main parts of your research.

60 second
summary

Does my research actually need charts? What software can I use to create my poster? This chapter offers helpful tips on the software you might
want to use to create your poster and also how you can visualize data to
present your research with the help of charts. Much the same way that
we think of the best metaphor to tell a story, we use data visualization
to illustrate different parts of our research. A chart is in itself a metaphor
and, as such, it can take different forms to represent different types of
data linked to (or generated) by our research. Not all research makes use
of data. But if you have data that could benefit from being represented
visually, check here how best to get your point across, and some tips on
how tools can make your life easier.

The elements of good data visualizations

When chosen and generated correctly, a chart can be a powerful tool for communication, but not all research makes use of charts. Nevertheless, a lot of researchers and students use them to represent different parts of their research visually (whether they use quantitative data or not in the actual analysis). When you make decisions about which information from your research could be represented visually with charts, consider these four things:

Information is about what you choose to represent as a chart. The amount of data you have available, as well as its quality, may influence how you choose to present your data. Even if your research builds on pre-existing data or generates a lot of new data, it is important to know that not all data should be included in the poster. **Actually, putting too many graphs on a poster will end up confusing your audience.**

Concept is the key message a chart communicates. It is the 'need to know' about your research. To decide what parts make up the concept, ask yourself this question: Is this relevant and essential for my poster? If yes, it probably belongs on your poster. If not, it is more in the 'nice to know' category. For example, if you want to represent the correlation between multiple variables, always use charts rather than the statistical output as a table generated by your statistical analysis software. Also, depending on the type of analysis, representing visually the relationships between a few key variables might be more telling than presenting to your audience a chart with all the variables and the values of their relationships.

Goal is the function that a certain graph plays, or rather, why it should be included. For instance, if that correlation is the best way to address your research question, you might want to use some text in the graph (in the legend or the title of the graph) to explain that.

Visual form is the visual metaphor you choose to get your point across. Should you use a bar chart or a map, or something else? In any case, the selection of the right visual metaphor to represent your data serves the important role of reducing the visual clutter and considering what your audience needs.

Which visualizations to use?

This section presents some of the most commonly used charts you can use, based on the type of data you have:

Highlighting a figure

An important number (for instance, a relevant percentage value) accompanied by explanatory information:

79%
Volume increase
from year one to year five

Proportional icons:

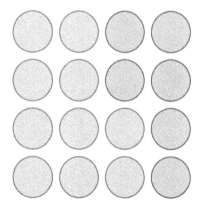

Comparing two or more variables

Bar chart

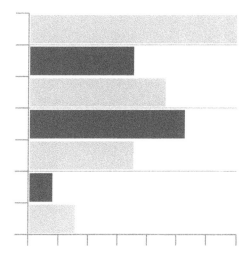

Side by side bars

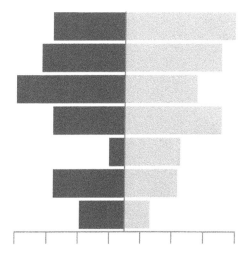

Radar or area chart

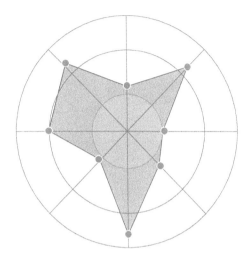

Stacked area chart

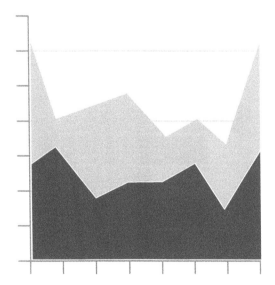

Compared to target bar chart

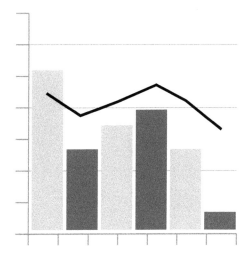

Parts of a whole

Tree map

Stacked area chart

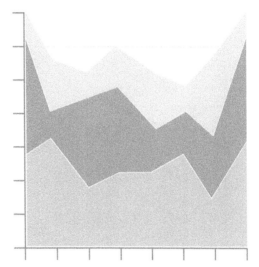

Nested elements

Stacked bars

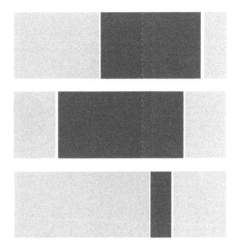

Correlation

Scatter plot chart

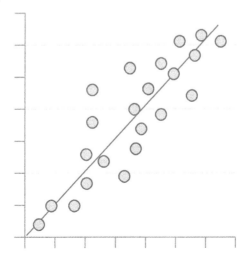

Relationship

Venn diagram

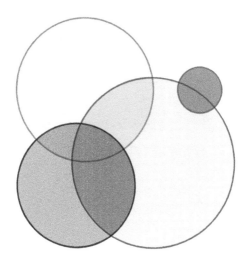

Network diagram

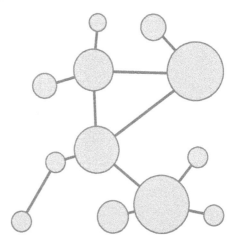

Comparing distribution

Histogram chart

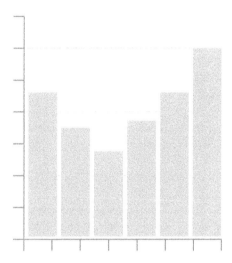

Bell curve

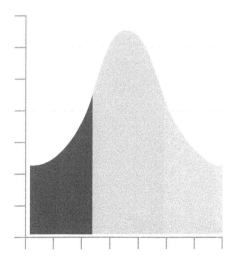

Dos

- Clear, easy-to-read labels and annotations help your data tell the story. But a graph should make sense by itself and should not need a lot of additional information for the audience to understand it.

- Choose a meaningful sorting strategy for your data, to make the most of outliers and patterns.

- Check the colour contrast. About 4.5% of people are colour blind.

- Start column charts/bars at zero (you would overemphasize the differences otherwise), and avoid using truncated axis, since they distort the relative size of the columns.

- Avoid pie charts and gauges, as much as possible. People are not very good at reading angles and proportions in circles, especially with small differences. Gauges take too much room to communicate very little, and aren't very indicative (often there is nothing to compare with).

- Steer clear of 3-D graphs and other unnecessary distractions that make data harder to read.

- Do not use two or more Y-axis in one chart. It makes for a misleading perception of the difference between elements.

'By visualizing information, we turn it into a landscape that you can explore with your eyes. A sort of information map. And when you're lost in information, an information map is kind of useful.'

David McCandless (2012)

ACTIVITY

Not all data can be best represented visually in a chart. The questions in this activity will help you decide if you need to use charts to present your research on a poster.

1   Do you use quantitative data in your research, whether to illustrate your research topic and the background for your research topic, or to carry out your analysis?

2   If yes, what type of data do you have?

  a   Comparative data (this can be nominal, ordinal, interval or ratio).

  b   Over-time data.

  c   Cross-sectional data.

  d   Do you have outliers?

  e   Are you carrying out inferential analysis?

  f   Are you using any data (also) for descriptive purposes?

Now you can decide **how** you want to represent the data visually with the help of a chart. Take a close look at the types of charts included earlier in this section and select one or two that you would like to use. Use the space below to write the reasons you have selected this particular chart, as best suited to represent the data you want to include on your poster.

- Type of chart

- Why is this chart best suited to represent visually the data I want to include on my poster?

Software for your poster

The digital tools you may use to create your poster evolve and change all the time (or new software is released), but as a rule of thumb, it is better to stick with something you are already familiar with.

Surprisingly, PowerPoint may be a pretty good option: you may be using it already, and it allows you to paste in Excel graphs.

Other options are:

- Impress (part of the LibreOffice suite) www.libreoffice.org/discover/impress/

- Keynote (Mac only) www.apple.com/uk/keynote/

- Google slides www.google.co.uk/slides/about/

We would not recommend using professional, vector-based publishing/design software unless you are very comfortable doing so, otherwise these can take a while to master and get acceptable results:

- Affinity Publisher https://affinity.serif.com/en-gb/publisher/

- Adobe InDesign www.adobe.com/uk/products/indesign.html

- Inkscape https://inkscape.org/

- Adobe Illustrator www.adobe.com/uk/products/illustrator.html

Generally, pixel-based software like Adobe Photoshop isn't advisable as it requires additional work to make a poster print-friendly, and the resulting file will be too large to handle easily.

Preparing your poster file using PowerPoint

1   Open a blank presentation with one slide, then select the Design tab near the upper right corner and select Slide size > Custom slide size (File > Page setup > Options > Paper size > Manage custom sizes on a Mac).

2   Select portrait/landscape and enter the dimensions (get guidance on size from your tutor) and click OK. If asked whether you want to maximize content or ensure fit, select the latter and click OK. Your poster file is now ready.

3   You can also find ready-made templates online (check the resources section at the end of the book).

Practical tips

- Once your poster is fully ready, make a copy and export it to PDF to send to print.

- Check with your printer which types of paper they have available and if needed, ask for advice on the best option for your poster.

- Order a print proof (A3 size may be OK if you can't get an actual size one) to make sure things look good on paper before you order the final version.

- Colour settings vary and what you see on your monitor will not look exactly the same on paper. Expect a shift in colour by two or three shades. Run a small proof to make sure.

- Remember not to link data or images from other applications. It is better to use drag & drop or copy & paste.

How do I tell the right story with my poster?

10 second
summary

A research poster tells the story of your journey to a wider audience, and here you will find out what you need to do to produce a compelling story with your own poster.

60 second summary

We are wired to respond to stories that join the dots for us. Narrative elements in a poster help your audience understand and remember the main messages you want to communicate about your research. Words are not the only material that matters for storytelling. Equally important is how we use colour and typography to visualize them. Yes, research in the social sciences follows clearly defined rules, but that does not mean that your poster has to be a cold list of disconnected facts and figures; think of it more as telling others how it all went, in a somewhat linear way. What do you want people to remember about your research? What could get in the way of understanding it? The use of language in combination with images, and what you decide to highlight can go a long way in helping you summarize your research experience in a compelling and memorable way.

Having a coherent narrative

Stories change greatly depending on how they are told. A biography could be turned into a comedy, a drama, a mystery and so on. But wouldn't it be confusing if each chapter belonged to a different genre? In Chapter 3, we saw how some basic rules can help us direct the audience's eyes towards what we want, and group elements that belong together. It is time to bring those elements to life and give them a voice.

Ensure that the story you tell accurately captures your research

- As in a conversation, the language you use should be easy to understand, even if some parts will inevitably be more technical. If you have a mixed audience, you may have to dial down the academic jargon so everyone is in step. Use plain language as much as possible and consider including a short glossary and/or examples if you think it may help your audience.

- Very long chunks of uniform text or small, complex graphs are much less engaging. When you decide what to include in your poster, it is easy to get carried away because everything seems important, but keep to the essentials and do not try to cram in too much, or else it may not be read.

  Narrative
  How a poster communicates in a way that all elements tie in with one another as we read through them.

- Break things down but make sure that they still make some sense by themselves. People may 'jump' bits when reading your poster quickly. Descriptive titles and separations (where possible) may help those who are not willing to read it all.

H1: likely to be read

I'm here to catch your eye

H2: may be read

And I'm here to tell you why you want to keep reading

H3: May be read

I'm here to separate sections

Body: Occasionally read

Lorem ipsum dolor sit amet, consectetur adipiscing elit, sed do eiusmod tempor incididunt ut labore et dolore magna aliqua. Ut enim ad minim veniam, quis nostrud exercitation ullamco laboris nisi ut aliquip ex ea commodo consequat.

Quote: likely to be read

"

Being a quote, I make things look smarter

Tidy up using hierarchies

- Last but not least, look for relatable ways to present your figures. Saying 'the uptake is 25%' isn't the same as 'one in four people use it', even though you are saying the same thing.

Colour and contrast

How you apply colour can make a big difference to making your poster easy on the eye. In Chapter 3 we saw how colour can impact prominence (the visual weight), so use it sparingly and to your advantage.

Do not use colour just because you can. For example, if you decide not to work with a white background (assuming it will be printed out on white paper), make sure there is a strong rationale for it. Otherwise things will be harder to read (it may smudge over the white text, etc.) and elements may be less readable.

Decide on a few colours and stick with them. Use contrast (varying the brightness of a given colour) to make things stand out. Colour should be consistent across your poster, as it will make it easier to navigate meaning and identify elements.

- Complementary colours maximize contrast.

- Use brightness to make things visible.

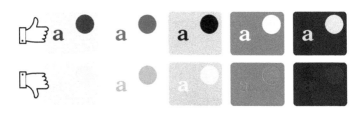

- Contrast between background and foreground to maximize readability.

- Ideally, graphs will use a common colour palette for a more cohesive look.

Typography and voice

Typography helps set the tone and the voice of your poster's content. Use it right and nobody will even notice it; use it the wrong way and it will make your poster confusing or hard to read. You do not need to be an expert designer (or spend lots of time deciding over fonts) to make the most of it.

We have learnt to associate fonts with different types of messaging. This can greatly impact how your content is read. For example, compare how the same sentence reads in the images below:

See you soon

SEE YOU SOON

SEE YOU SOON

So, unless you want to apply a very specific effect or voice (on a headline or quote), it is better to stick to a rather neutral, standard font. For example, when sharing your poster as a file online or via email, it will look different (possibly disjointed) if the receiver does not have your poster's fonts in their device.

Typography
The use of typefaces and text to communicate a message in a clear and appealing way.

Voice
The tone of a message in a given context. For instance, warm and informal, as opposed to technical and direct.

Tip!

- Weight: Use different weights, such as thin, light, heavy or black, but keep it to one font: mixing fonts requires some knowledge to pair them well, and you don't want the attention on that, but on your content.

- Contrast: Subtle changes in font weight and size can make it hard for people to tell the difference. Make sure there is enough contrast between different types of text.

- Times New Roman, Georgia, Verdana, Arial or Tahoma are good fonts, in that they are all pretty versatile and standardized.

- Fonts where the stroke is very irregular become harder to read at small sizes, because the thinner parts become less visible and the eyes need to make an extra effort. Take a look at Bodoni and Georgia to compare.

Bodoni

ABC abc *abc* **abc**

Georgia

ABC abc *abc* **abc**

- Be mindful of the line height and line width for better legibility. Optimal line length is said to be around 50 to 60 characters per line, including spaces.

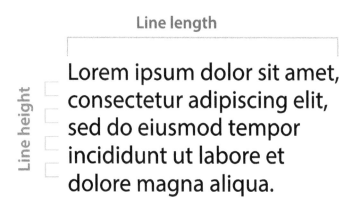

- Make sure no text is too small for your audience to read.

ACTIVITY Observation

Look for images of research posters online, pick one and check how it fares on the themes outlined in this chapter. Which things are good, and which are bad?

- Does it present a coherent and compelling narrative?

- Does it make good use of colour and contrast?

- Does it make good use of typography?

ACTIVITY The interrogatory

Start with one of the main themes of your research, then imagine you want to question everything about it:

- Why should my audience care?

- How could I best illustrate the theme visually?

- How can I best integrate this theme into the whole story that my poster is telling?

- Is there a hierarchy I want to use?

- How can I use colour and contrast to fit the theme into the poster?

- Could typography help me integrate the theme in the poster?

Repeat it with other themes in your research. With this exercise, it is fine if you go off-topic, because it is about generating lots of answers only to refine them later, selecting only what proves relevant enough to be included in the poster.

'Whatever we do, if not understood, fails to communicate and is wasted effort.'

– Massimo Vignelli (2010), p.14

A student told us

'My research has a lot of facts and figures collected over a long time and it isn't easy to summarize.'

A lot can be said with very little; your poster does not need to be a full account of your entire research journey but a compilation of highlights that sum up the story for your audience in a cohesive way.

- Research writing is best when it is clear and direct; use the same kind of language and style in your poster.

- Apply a consistent hierarchy to your elements, so the audience can easily find information when they look at your poster.

- Colour is used with a purpose and, when used right, it does not get in the way of legibility (especially if you need to print out your poster).

- Text is best used when it is clear, tidy and comfortable to read, even in small sizes.

How do I use images?

10 second
summary

Images can be very powerful, but with
great power comes great responsibility.
Make sure you make the best of them
to enhance your poster the right way,
both in a practical and conceptual way.

60 second summary

Images communicate differently from words. In the context of a poster, it is best to select images that form a coherent group (with themselves and the other elements), to help you convey the right message about your research in the right way. Images should have a purpose and not be used simply as space fillers, nor should they look disconnected. If they are the wrong size or resolution, you will not print as good quality images and, as such, will give an overall negative impression of the entire poster. In this section we will go over a few basics to make good use of images on your poster (be they photos, illustrations, etc.).

'Seeing comes before words. The child looks and recognises before it can speak.'

–John Berger (1972)

Choosing relevant images, illustrations or charts

Not only do we spot images faster than we read text, but our eyes are naturally drawn to images because of their evocative quality. Whatever pictures and illustrations (or graphs) you use, they will be the first thing others notice when they look at your poster, using them to make a (sub-conscious) choice on whether or not the rest of the information on the poster may be of interest. This does not mean that images are the only elements that will inform that split-second decision, but they are very important nonetheless. Images help to 'set the tone' for the entire poster.

Even if it isn't always possible to align all images of a poster perfectly, your poster can have:

- **Charts and illustrations** of the same style and colour palette (or very similar), which actually support your poster's content and/or make it easier to read (think simple icons on a list for example).

- **Photographs** that make sense in the context of your research and clearly illustrate a concept or part of the analysis to which you are referring in your research. Using generic and decorative stock pictures is rarely a good idea.

Last but not least, pictures, graphs, etc. should support your narrative (not distract people from it), and be supported by an easily legible caption.

Think of which parts of your research would need to be supported by visuals the most when turned into a poster. What (photographs, illustrations, graphs) would be the most helpful to illustrate each of those parts? Use the table below to write down which parts of your research you want to represent visually in your poster by using images. You can also write down the exact source/title of each image, so you can easily find this when you need it.

Part of research project/Type of image	Photographs	Illustrations	Graphs
Research puzzle			
Research 'gap'			
Research method			
Data			
Research findings			
Contribution to knowledge			

Some technical basics

You will probably create your poster on a computer, then print it out. Bear in mind that what you see on the screen will look different on paper, as the two versions are created differently.

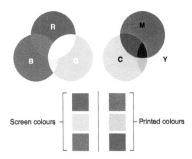

Screen colours — | | — Printed colours

- Screens work by adding light, using a mixture of Red, Green and Blue (RGB), and the elements of images are made from pixels.

- Printers subtract light instead, using Cyan, Magenta, Yellow and Black (CMYK), adding dots of ink on paper to recreate elements.

This basically means colours will print out less bright than they appear on the screen and things may need resizing. If you can, export a copy of your final poster to CMYK mode, and run a print test to make sure it is all visible and readable.

An image is made out of pixels on the screen (left), and dots of ink when printed (right).

Size vs resolution

Often size and resolution are considered to be the same thing. This is a common misconception, but these two are in fact not the same.

- **Resolution** is about density and is commonly measured in DPI (dots per inch, as traditionally the printer adds dots of ink to form an image, where more dots mean a sharper image).

  Resolution
  The quality of an image or graphic element. A higher resolution indicates higher definition.

- **Size** refers to the dimensions of the image. Images with the same size can come in different resolutions.

180 DPI   72 DPI

32 DPI   12 DPI

The effect of higher vs lower resolution. Regular monitors used to work at 72 DPI, but many go over 200 DPI nowadays. For reference, commercial artwork is usually designed to be printed at 300 DPI and above.

A student told us

'After working on the poster for so long, it is hard to imagine what it will look like once printed.'

Remember the size and resolution of an on-screen element can be very different once printed. Again, early print tests are always a good idea if you're unsure.

Vectors vs rasterized images

Even if what we see are just pixels, computers can also render images and text as vectors (lines between anchor points). The main advantages of vector images are their scalability and how crisp they look once printed, as they are perfect curves rather than pixels. A common format for these is SVG (Scalable Vector Graphics).

An element made out of vectors (left) vs an element made out of pixels (right).

Be mindful of text and graphs/charts if you need to rasterize them, especially when working from Photoshop or other raster-based applications: you will need to convert text layers to vector shapes before exporting for print, and if you do not keep a copy of the original you will lose the ability to edit such text.

On other software, such as PowerPoint, letters in text and shapes are usually rendered as vectors by default.

SVG format
Image format based on vectors instead of pixels, where elements can be resized with no loss of quality.

CHECK
LIST

By now, you will have made most of the important decisions about the content of your poster and should have also selected the images that you want to include. Take each image and make sure to do a print test. You can use the checklist below for the images in your poster, to make certain that each image is formatted well and looks its best. If you have more than three images in your poster, you can copy the same table below onto a separate sheet of paper:

	Image 1	Image 2	Image 3
Are the colours in each printed image clear enough?			
Is this image the right resolution?			
Is this image the right size?			
If it is a graph, can it be exported to SVG format?			

Congratulations

You have learned a huge amount so far, so take a moment to congratulate yourself on all the knowledge you have acquired about the main principles of research design and poster design needed to create a research poster. You know the main concepts, you have practised these, and have also made some key decisions about how you can apply them to your own research poster.

Now you are ready to bring everything together and finalize the work needed to create a great research poster.

How do I know if my poster is good?

10 second summary

This section will give you different checklists and templates to help you make decisions about the content of your poster and to enable you to design a good poster.

60 second summary

Posters are made of distinct elements, and to create a great poster, you need to link them all together successfully. At this point, this is not difficult to do, as you have learned a lot about different parts of a good research poster. This section gives you practical guidance on how to create your research poster, integrating all the elements of research design and poster design in a visually cohesive and appealing composition. Additionally, this section will help you assess whether or not your poster is good as you are approaching the end of the design process.

Plan for attention time

People will 'experience' your poster at walking speed, so they will need to be able to understand what's on your poster very quickly, in a matter of seconds. Think of your poster more as a 'billboard' that must rapidly achieve two main things:

- Maximizes insight, so a person looking at your poster will be able to get the gist of your research relatively quickly, and without needing to read a lot of text and engage in a great deal of conversation with you, to make sense of the information displayed.

- Only includes the essential items.

. . . .

. . . .

. . . .

. . . .

. . . .

Need to know (come first) vs nice to know (come last)

- The 'need to know' might vary, depending on the stage of research you are at. If you already have findings, the first thing that your audience **needs to know** about is **the main finding(s)** of your research. If you are at an earlier stage of research, you can select your research question, the main argument or perhaps your main hunch or expectation of your analysis, based on existing studies on the same topics or on related topics.

- Place this 'need to know' information front and centre in your poster!

- Use plain language as much as possible to present your main finding(s).

- Do you have a graph or an illustration for this 'need to know' information? If so, include it centrally somewhere in your poster.

- 'Nice to know' information can be included in the poster and can be located farther away from the central column.

- **The principle of progressive disclosure**: For more information on your research, especially if you are an advanced student or have completed your research, you can consider adding a QR code and further links to your paper, so people can access more information about your work. You can very easily generate QR codes on the internet (see the resources section), and any smartphone will be able to read these.

A checklist of the main research design elements

- How much of my research have I completed/carried out as I start designing my poster? What do I feel comfortable sharing with others on a poster?

  - Research interest/topic.

  - 'Gap' in scholarship.

  - Research question.

  - A body of academic work to which I aim to contribute.

  - Research hypotheses/research expectations and argument (as relevant for my research).

  - Method of data collection and methodology.

  - Data, and method of analysis (if applicable).

  - Analysis and discussion of findings.

  - Conclusion.

Group the information in the previous list in two separate lists, based on priority, to help you decide how to organize the information on your poster. Essentially, this decision is informed by how much of your research you have completed:

- The 'need to know'

....

....

....

....

- The 'nice to know'

....

....

....

....

A checklist of the key principles of poster design

How can I best represent visually on a poster the above elements?

- Where should I position 'the need to know' on the poster?

- What colours, if any, should I use?

- Can I use an image?

- If there is text, what font size should I use? And which font?

- Which composition principles should I apply?

 Prototype

Try applying what you have learned from the previous sections of this book to quickly mock up a final version of your poster on a sheet of paper or your computer. Plan for types of content, their placement and hierarchies, etc.

'Creating a poster is like cooking. Choose a dish that you know well, find the right ingredients, and get cooking, using the right methods and the right tools. Then, your guests will love it.'

Main elements of assessment of a research poster

If you are presenting your poster as part of a course or as part of the preparation for your dissertation, you will most likely be given a set of criteria for assessing your poster and marking it, as appropriate for each course and university/institution of higher education. Your instructor will be interested in whether or not you have carried out your research and can continue to do so, while integrating the feedback you receive at the poster session. Assessment criteria will likely also mention the importance of clarity and conciseness in the presentation of the information on your poster.

Remember that a good poster is one that communicates your research **successfully** to your audience. This entails using a **clear**, **concise**, and **accessible** style of poster design that visually guides the audience away from what they **need to know** towards what they might also want to know about your research.

A student told us

'I felt more insecure about my poster the more I worked on it.'

If this is you, don't worry. It is completely normal to feel this way. The truth is the more you learn, the more you become aware of the factors you need to consider. That also means you can plan for and control them.

Congratulations

By now all the elements of your poster are in place, and your poster is ready for printing. Take a moment to congratulate yourself on the great work you have accomplished so far. Now you are ready for the final stage of planning – thinking about how you will be presenting your poster to your audience.

How do I integrate my research poster in a good presentation?

10 second summary

Often, you will be asked to present your poster and/or address questions about it, and this section offers advice on how to prepare well for such situations.

60 second summary

The content and images you have included in the poster will 'speak for themselves', inspiring people to learn more about your research and ask more questions. You might be asked to be present in the room where your poster will be exhibited, standing close to it, and to perhaps even give a brief presentation that will help the audience understand your research better. Even if you do not need to give a presentation, you will likely be expected to address questions that the audience might have about the various information you have included in your poster. This chapter offers lots of useful tips about how you can use your research poster as a presentation aid, and how you can encourage the audience to engage with your poster in a meaningful way.

Use your research poster as a presentation aid

By now, you will have a well-designed research poster and are probably feeling confident about its content and general design. You might have already printed your poster and are therefore ready to have it on display for others to learn about your research.

In Section 4, you were encouraged to find out details about the context in which you will be displaying your research poster. By now, you will surely have all the details about the venue, the lighting, the audience. When you learned all of the above, you were probably also told whether or not you would be expected to introduce your poster to the audience by giving a presentation. You might only need to stand near your poster and address questions, if audience members want to learn more about your research and the information you have included.

To plan for the actual day(s) when your poster will be on display, you will need answers to the following questions from the event organizers. This information may have already been shared with you from the start of your work on the poster or at some point during the poster creation process. If it was not given to you, please make sure you find out those answers by consulting the event details (on the event website or in other promotional materials) or by asking the organizers and/or other participants who have reliable information about the event.

Remember!

You will be presenting your research to people, not your poster. The former allows you to weave a story, the latter sums it up. **And nobody in the room knows more about your research than you do.**

You might be expected to:

Introduce yourself or another colleague:

- Do I need to introduce myself to the audience or will someone else introduce me?

- If an introduction is needed, how many minutes do I have for this introduction?

- What type or information is usually shared in such an introduction?

Introduce the poster and its contents:

- How many minutes do I have to introduce the contents of my poster and speak about my research?

- What is the expected level of detail in such a presentation?

- Am I expected to make this presentation interactive, by asking the audience questions?

Address questions from the audience:

- Will I be present when the audience will look at my poster?

- If so, will I be expected to address questions in a dedicated Q&A session, or more spontaneously, as people looking at my poster address me?

Use the spaces below to write (in bullet point format) the main information and ideas you want to share with the audience, if you are asked to introduce yourself and/or your poster and research.

Introduce yourself:

Introduce your poster and its contents:

What questions do you think you might be asked, and how will you answer those questions?

Remember!

Your audience will most likely have to look at several other posters in a relatively short amount of time. Sometimes, poster sessions can include tens or even hundreds of research posters, and many of them might indeed contain very important findings for other researchers to learn about. When you introduce yours, make sure that you focus on what your audience '**needs to know**' about your research, which is often your main finding(s). Try your best to explain this information in plain and accessible language. When possible, use a main illustration or graph, to help your audience visualize the key information about your research. If anyone is interested in learning more about your work, they will approach you with questions. Then, you can offer more details about your research project.

A student told us

'I get nervous when I have to speak in front of an audience.'

If you get nervous when you present in front of an audience (and most people tend to feel nervous!), you might find it helpful to bring the notes you made on the previous page to the event itself, so you can consult them as needed. If nerves tend to keep you from remembering questions or suggestions from the audience, take a pen and paper and write them down. You can consult these later, when you address them, and even after the event is finished.

Engage in (and encourage audience) interaction with the poster

Here are some key tips that will help you on the day of the event.

- Stand beside the poster (not in front of it!).

- Give your audience time to read and examine the poster closely before you approach them to see if they have any questions.

- Whether you are presenting your research or just answering questions about it, make sure that you show your audience how best to 'read' your poster, by following the logical thread of the information's organization.

- Feel free to point at images and information on the poster, to visually guide the audience towards the right information.

- Body language is important, so try your best to relax and smile as you are presenting or when a member of the audience approaches you and looks at your poster.

- Do your best to enjoy your time at the event.

- Try to keep an open mind about new ideas and suggestions from the audience. You are there both to share your research and to learn from others. Write these down, so you can think about them later as well. When a question or a suggestion is not clear, you can ask for clarification.

- Sometimes when you attend a poster session, you will not get asked any questions. This is perfectly normal and a common occurrence too. It does not mean your research is not interesting. Remember that your audience will be looking at a lot of research posters in a short amount of time, so they will often not have enough time to engage with every poster in the room, no matter how fascinating the research might be. It could be that the design of your poster is 'too busy', thus making it hard for the audience to make sense of it in a short amount of time. However, if you follow the advice in this book you will design a great research poster, so you will definitely avoid this problem!

CHECK
LIST

Finally, here are some practical questions about logistics. You should find out the answers to these questions a few days prior to the event where you will be presenting your research poster:

- Do I have to arrive early at the venue to (help) set up my poster?

- If so, do I need to bring any tools (i.e. clips, pins, Blu Tack, etc.)?

- Am I expected to stay until after the event has ended, to remove my research poster from the display and the venue?

> 'Perfection is not when you have nothing to add, it is when you have nothing to take away.'
>
> - Antoine de Saint Exupéry (1939)

You have worked hard to create an excellent research poster and share it with your audience. Well done – now it's time to celebrate!

Final checklist: How to know you are done

Tick all the statements you completed as you created you research poster:

I know why I need to create a research poster
and how it will benefit me. ❏

I am aware of the elements of my research I have completed
and which ones I want to include in the research poster. ❏

I understand what makes a research poster
good (or not so good). ❏

I have all the information I need before I start creating
my poster – details about the venue/space, specific event
requirements, specified content and formatting details for
posters, and assessment criteria. ❏

I understand how and why I should use graphs to represent my research visually. ☐

I feel confident that I can tell a compelling, concise, and coherent story about the research included on my poster. ☐

I know how I can integrate images in my poster and why they are important to illustrate the main elements of my research. ☐

I feel confident that I can assess whether my poster is good (or still needs further work). ☐

I have a solid understanding of how to give a presentation about my poster. ☐

Glossary

Narrative   How a poster communicates in a way that all elements tie in with one another as we read through them.

Qualitative data   Generally non-numerical data obtained by the researcher from first-hand observation, interviews, questionnaires, focus groups, participant-observation, recordings made in natural settings, documents, and artifacts.

Quantitative data   Numerical data that can be statistically analysed.

Research design   The overall strategy that researchers use to integrate different components of a study in a coherent and logical way.

Research question   A question that a research project sets out to answer.

Resolution The quality of an image or graphic element. A higher resolution indicates higher definition.

SVG format Image format based on vectors instead of pixels, where elements can be resized with no loss of quality.

Typography The use of typefaces and text to communicate a message in a clear and appealing way.

Visual weight The notion that factors like colour or size can render design elements more visually prominent than others.

Voice The tone of a message in a given context. For instance, warm and informal, as opposed to technical and direct.

Further Resources

Charts

Charticulator

https://charticulator.com/

Libre Office Charts

www.libreoffice.org/discover/charts/

Templates

Templates in various formats and sizes www.posterpresentations.com/free-poster-templates.html

Use of images online

Quick guide on the right to use images https://thevisualcommunicationguy.com/2014/07/14/can-i-use-that-picture/

Generating QR codes

Online tool to generate codes

www.barcode-generator.org/

A tool to generate codes in Android

https://github.com/JiashuWu/Android-Barcode

References

Antoine de Saint Exupéry (1939) *Wind, Sand and Stars*. New York: Reynal & Hitchcock.

Berger, J. (1972) *Ways of Seeing.* London: BBC and Penguin.

McCandless, D. (2012) 'The beauty of data visualization' [Video]. TED Conferences. www.youtube.com/watch?v=5Zg-C8AAlGg&feature=emb_title

Vignelli, M. (2010) *The Vignelli Canon*. Baden: Lars Müller Publishers.

Zeldman, J. (2008) 'Content precedes design', Zeldman on Web and Interaction Design. www.zeldman.com/2008/05/06/content-precedes-design/